COLOURS AROUND ME

Red

Anita Loughrey

QED Publishing

What is red?

Red is a colour.

This is the colour red.

Look at the picture of the pond.

What can you see on the pond that is red?

Answer: The boat is red.

Finding red

Point to the things that are red.

STOP

How many red things can you see?

Matching red

Look at the apples on the tree.

Point to the two red apples.

Let's go shopping

Help the red car through the maze to get to the shop.

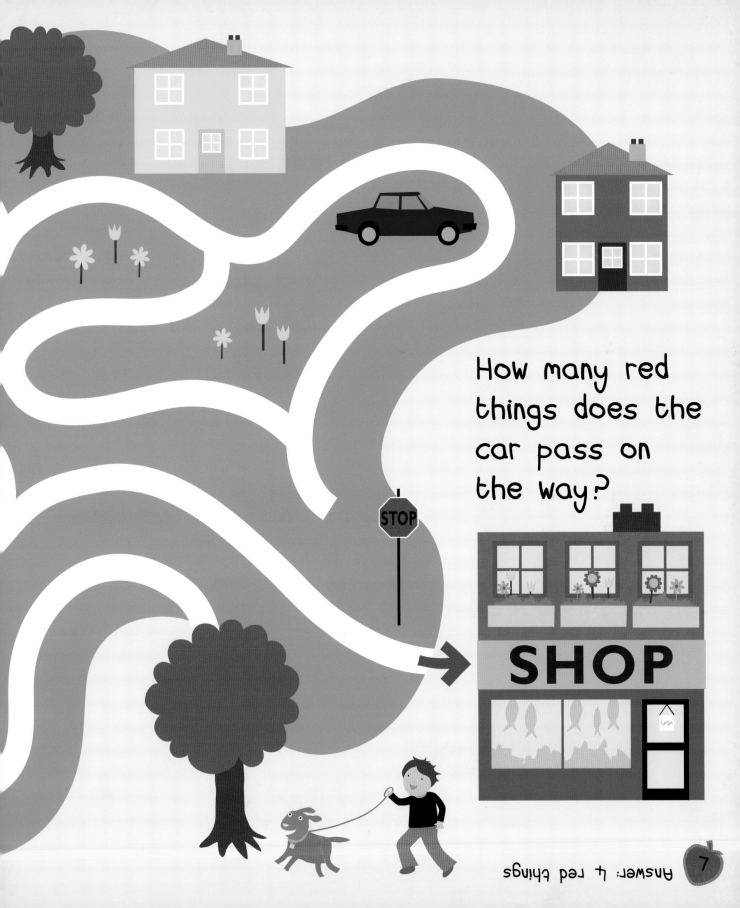

How many red things does the car pass on the way?

STOP

SHOP

Answer: 4 red things

Red shapes

Red things can be different shapes.

How many
red squares
can you see?

How many
red circles
can you see?

Answer: 2 red squares, 3 red circles

How many red rectangles
can you see?

How
many red
triangles can
you see?

What red shapes can
you see around you?

Answer: 2 red rectangles, 3 red triangles

Big and small

Red things can be different sizes.

big

bigger

small

biggest

smaller

smallest

Odd ones out

Some things here
are the wrong colour.

rose

banana

tree

dog

bird

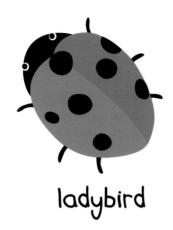

ladybird

strawberry

sunflower

lorry

clover

which things
should be red?

Answer: The rose, the ladybird and the strawberry should be red.

Shades of red

Red can be different shades.

dark red

dark red

red and dark red

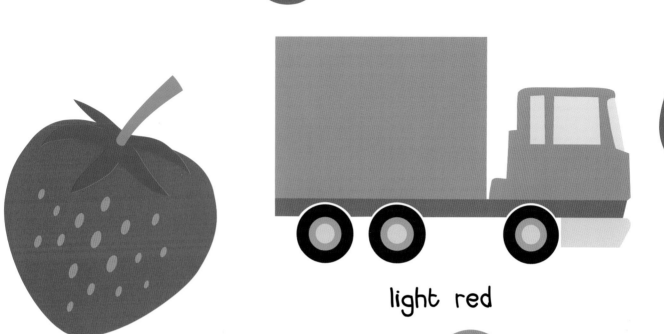

red

light red

light red

What shades of red can you see around you?

Red in the garden

Can you find these red things in the garden?

flowers

cherries

red ant

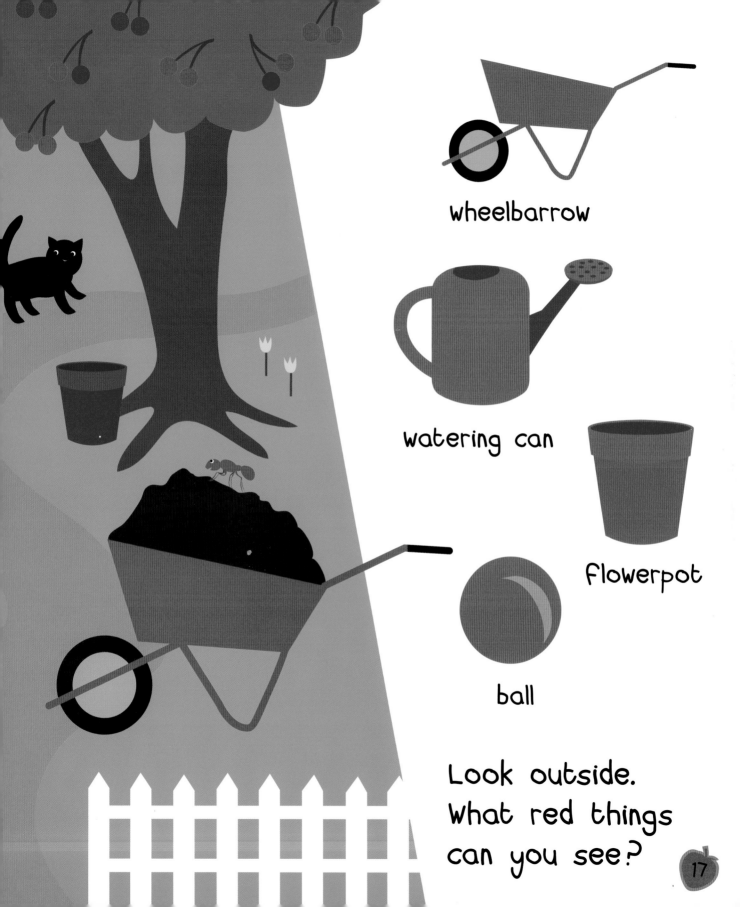

wheelbarrow

watering can

flowerpot

ball

Look outside.
What red things
can you see?

Red at the market

Point to all the red fruits you can see at the market.

apple

strawberry

plum

raspberry

20p

10p

30

20p

£1.50

tomato

pepper

watermelon

What other
fruits can
you think of
that are red?

£1

20p

20p

40p

Red is a warning

Red is used to tell us to be careful.

no entry sign

road barrier

cone

STOP

stop sign

fire engine

traffic light

brake lights

Have you ever seen any
of these red things?

21

Red is for love

Can you find these red things in the picture?

Happy Birthday, Mum

roses

present

birthday card

candles

chocolate box

necklace

shoes

What red-coloured things have you been given as presents?

Notes for parents and teachers

This book has been designed to help children to recognize the colour red and to distinguish red from other colours. The vibrant activities make learning fun and use the environment around them to reinforce what they have learned.

• Read the instructions to the child. Allow time for the child to think about the activity. Encourage them to discuss what they see.

• Praise the child if they recognize the items in the book. If any of the items are unfamiliar, explain what they are and where they might be found.

• If possible, take the child into the environment you have talked about so that they can observe items pictured in this book. Encourage the child to spot red objects using ideas from this book.

• Remember to keep it fun. Stop before the child gets tired or loses interest, then continue on another day. Children learn best when they are relaxed and enjoying themselves. It is best to help them experience new concepts in small steps.

Other activities you could try:

• Play games such as 'I spy': saying "I spy with my little eye a red thing beginning with...". If the child is not yet familiar with the alphabet, you could say the initial sound of the word rather than the letter name.

• Cut pictures from catalogues and magazines of different-coloured objects and ask the child to sort them, or match them to the pictures in this book.

• Ask the child what red things they can see when you are outside, at home, or looking in other books.

• Experiment with colour using different media such as paint, crayons, pastels and coloured paper.

Illustrator: Sue Hendra
Editor: Lauren Taylor
Designer: Fiona Hajée
Educational consultant: Jillian Harker

Copyright © QED Publishing 2011

First published in the UK in 2011 by
QED Publishing
A Quarto Group company
226 City Road
London EC1V 2TT

www.qed-publishing.co.uk

A catalogue record for this book is available from the British Library.

ISBN 978 1 84835 534 7

Printed in China